ROCK-OLOGY
The Hard Facts
About Rocks

What Is the Rock Cycle?

by Ellen Lawrence

Consultants:

Shawn W. Wallace
Department of Earth and Planetary Sciences
American Museum of Natural History, New York, New York

Kimberly Brenneman, PhD
National Institute for Early Education Research, Rutgers University
New Brunswick, New Jersey

BEARPORT
PUBLISHING

New York, New York

Credits

Cover, © Jason and Bonnie Grower/Shutterstock, © Siim Sepp/Shutterstock, © Leene/Shutterstock, and © John Foxx/Stockbyte/Thinkstock; 2, © sonsam/Shutterstock; 3T, © Tyler Boyes/Shutterstock; 3B, © Siim Sepp/Shutterstock; 4, © michal812/Shutterstock, © Fablok/Shutterstock, and © Gyvafoto/Shutterstock; 4–5, © BGSmith/Shutterstock; 6, © Paul B. Moore/Shutterstock; 6L, © marmo81/Shutterstock; 6C, © PerseoMedusa/Shutterstock; 6R, © Zacarias Pereira da Mata/Shutterstock; 8, © Siim Sepp/Shutterstock; 9, © Shutterstock; 10T, © Siim Sepp/Shutterstock; 10C, © Fredy Thuerig/Shutterstock; 10B, © Tyler Boyes/Shutterstock and © Rob Kemp/Shutterstock; 11, © Shutterstock; 12, © Elena Marzo/Shutterstock; 13, © Shutterstock; 14L, © michal812/Shutterstock; 14R, © sonsam/Shutterstock; 15, © Shutterstock; 15R, © Siim Sepp/Shutterstock; 16L, © Tyler Boyes/Shutterstock; 16R, © Siim Sepp/Shutterstock; 17L, © Shutterstock; 17TR, © John Copland/Shutterstock; 17BR, © Zadiraka Evgenii/Shutterstock; 18, © beboy/Shutterstock; 19, © arousa/Shutterstock; 20, © Michael Rosskothen/Shutterstock; 21, © Siim Sepp/Shutterstock, © Elena Marzo/Shutterstock, © tiverylucky/Shutterstock, © Keith Levit/Shutterstock, and © beboy/Shutterstock; 22, © Ruby Tuesday Books; 23TL, © ChameleonsEye/Shutterstock; 23TC, © Keith Levit/Shutterstock; 23TR, © LesPalenik/Shutterstock; 23BL, © Kevin Eng/Shutterstock; 23BC, © Marko Poplasen/Shutterstock; 23BR, © Dziewul/Shutterstock.

Publisher: Kenn Goin
Editorial Director: Adam Siegel
Creative Director: Spencer Brinker
Project Editor: Natalie Lunis
Photo Researcher: Ruby Tuesday Books Ltd

Library of Congress Cataloging-in-Publication Data

Lawrence, Ellen, 1967– author.
  What is the rock cycle? / by Ellen Lawrence.
      pages cm. — (Rock-ology)
  Audience: Ages 7–12.
  Includes bibliographical references and index.
  ISBN 978-1-62724-304-9 (library binding) — ISBN 1-62724-304-6 (library binding)
  1. Petrology—Juvenile literature. 2. Geochemical cycles—Juvenile literature. 3. Rocks—Juvenile literature.
I. Title.
  QE432.2.L396 2015
  552—dc23
                                    2014014021

For more information, write to Bearport Publishing Company, Inc., 45 West 21st Street, Suite 3B, New York, New York 10010. Printed in the United States of America.

10 9 8 7 6 5 4 3 2 1

Contents

Recycling Rocks

Rocks are all around us—in backyards, on beaches, and in high, rugged mountains.

Most of these rocks are millions of years old.

Yet no matter how old they are, rocks don't always stay the same.

In fact, old rocks are changing into new rocks all the time.

The way that old rocks are recycled into new ones is called the **rock cycle**.

How does the rock cycle work?

sandstone

marble

granite

There are thousands of different kinds of rocks. For example, sandstone, marble, and granite are three different kinds of rocks.

Look for rocks in a garden, in a park, or at the beach. Try to find three rocks that look very different from one another. Draw a picture of your rocks.

5

Three Main Types

Scientists group all the rocks on Earth into three main types.

They are called **igneous**, **sedimentary**, and **metamorphic** rock.

Each type of rock forms in a different way.

There are new igneous, sedimentary, and metamorphic rocks forming all the time.

The way that these rock types form is part of the rock cycle.

The scientific study of Earth's rocks is called geology. Scientists who study rocks are called geologists.

Granite is a kind of igneous rock.

Sandstone is a kind of sedimentary rock.

Marble is a kind of metamorphic rock.

Imagine that you are a geologist. Choose one of the pictures and describe the rock.

How Does Igneous Rock Form?

Igneous rock can form in two different ways.

The first way happens deep underground inside Earth's rocky crust.

Beneath the crust, there is super-hot liquid rock called **magma**.

Sometimes magma oozes up into cracks in the crust.

Then the liquid rock cools and hardens and becomes igneous rock.

gabbro

pegmatite

Gabbro and pegmatite are two kinds of igneous rock that form inside Earth's crust.

Igneous Rock Forming Underground

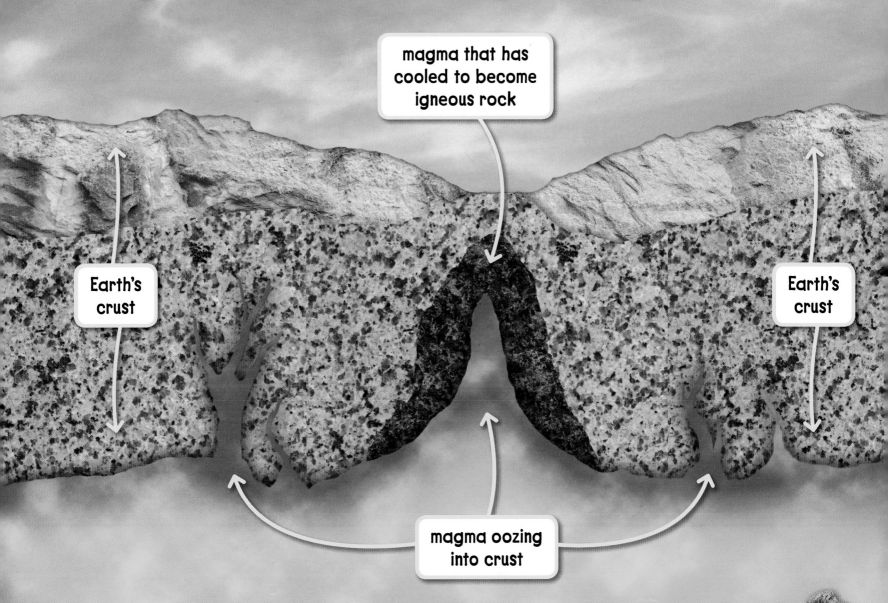

magma that has cooled to become igneous rock

Earth's crust

Earth's crust

magma oozing into crust

Rock from Volcanoes

The second way that igneous rock forms happens on Earth's surface.

Sometimes a large hole or crack, called a volcano, appears in Earth's crust.

Magma escapes from the volcano onto Earth's surface.

Once magma is on the surface, it is known as lava.

The super-hot lava cools, hardens, and becomes igneous rock.

lava flowing from a volcano

lava that has cooled and become igneous rock

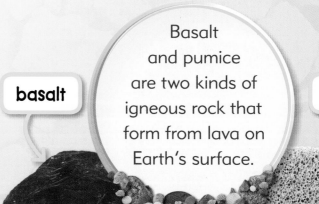

basalt

Basalt and pumice are two kinds of igneous rock that form from lava on Earth's surface.

pumice

Igneous Rock Forming Above the Ground

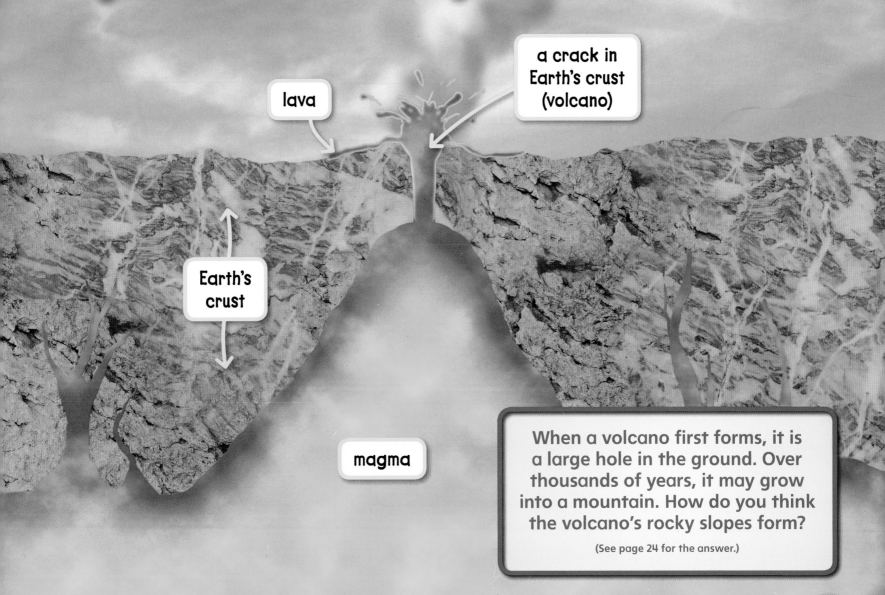

lava

a crack in Earth's crust (volcano)

Earth's crust

magma

When a volcano first forms, it is a large hole in the ground. Over thousands of years, it may grow into a mountain. How do you think the volcano's rocky slopes form?

(See page 24 for the answer.)

Recycling Igneous Rock

Igneous rock may not stay the same forever.

The rock on a volcano's slopes can change into a new type of rock.

How?

When it rains, water flows down the volcano's rocky slopes and loosens pieces of rock.

The loose pieces are carried down the volcano by rainwater.

Then they are washed into a river.

Pieces of rock that break off from a larger rock are called **sediment**. Some pieces of sediment are as tiny as grains of table salt.

What do you think might happen next to the loose pieces of rock?

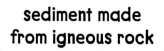

sediment made from igneous rock

Making Sedimentary Rock

The rocky sediment from the volcano's slopes is carried by a river into a lake.

Here, the rocky pieces settle on the bottom.

Over thousands of years, more sediment is washed into the lake.

Layer upon layer of tiny rocky pieces build up.

After millions of years, the layers of sediment join together and become new sedimentary rock.

Sandstone and conglomerate are kinds of sedimentary rock. Conglomerate rock contains pieces of sediment in many different sizes.

conglomerate

sandstone

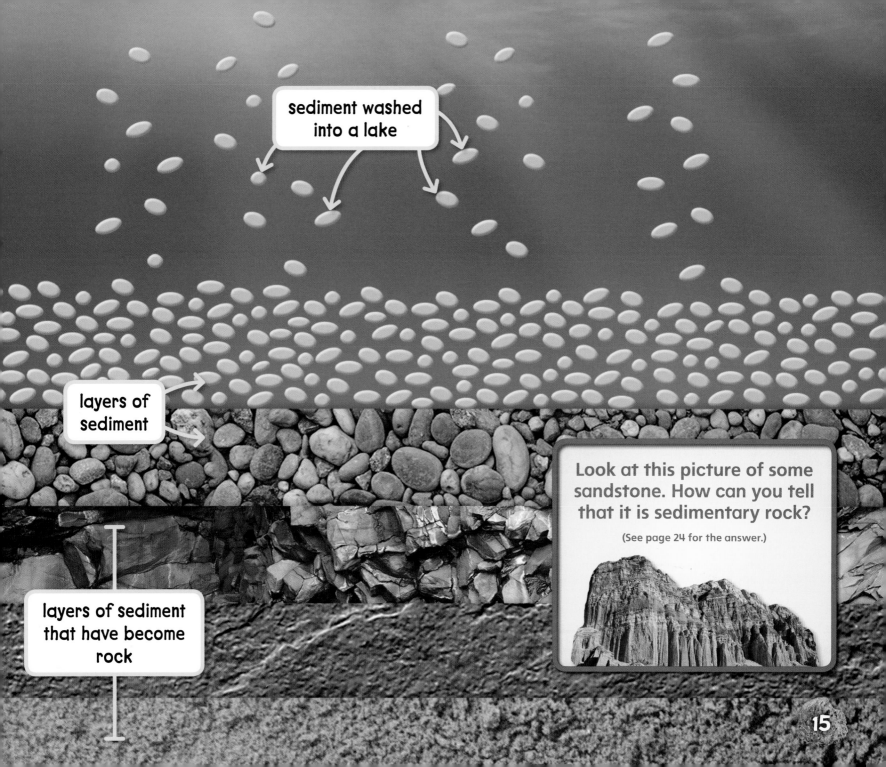

sediment washed into a lake

layers of sediment

layers of sediment that have become rock

Look at this picture of some sandstone. How can you tell that it is sedimentary rock?

(See page 24 for the answer.)

Recycling Sedimentary Rock

Sedimentary rock may not stay the same forever.

Sometimes Earth's crust cracks and moves.

As the crust moves, rocks are crushed, stretched, folded, and rubbed against each other.

These movements create lots of heat, which bakes the rocks.

Being crushed and baked changes sedimentary rock into metamorphic rock.

Sometimes movements in Earth's crust cause igneous rock to be crushed and baked. Then igneous rock can change into metamorphic rock, too.

schist
(metamorphic rock)

basalt
(igneous rock)

changes into

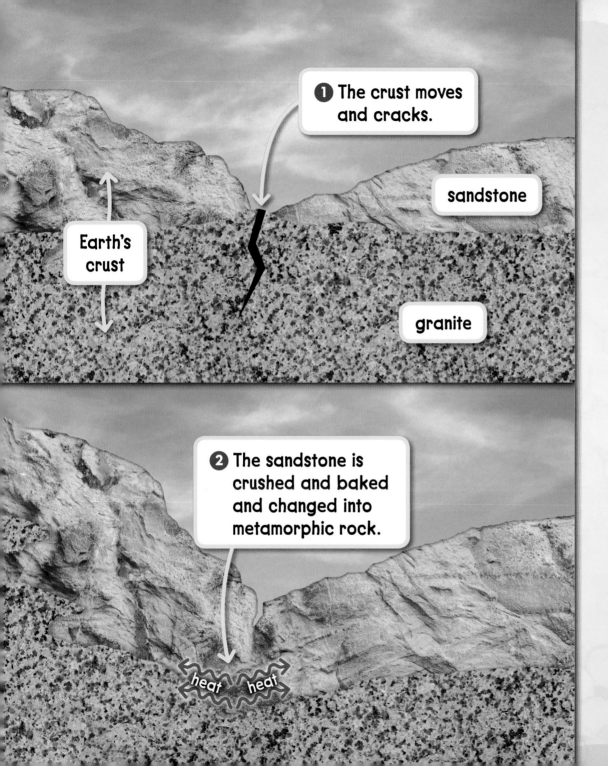

❶ The crust moves and cracks.

Earth's crust

sandstone

granite

❷ The sandstone is crushed and baked and changed into metamorphic rock.

heat   heat

When sandstone is crushed and baked, it becomes quartzite.

sandstone
(sedimentary rock)

changes into

quartzite
(metamorphic rock)

From Rock to Magma

Just like other types of rock, metamorphic rock can change into something new.

Sometimes, when Earth's crust moves, metamorphic rock in the crust cracks.

Then, super-hot magma oozes into the crack and heats the rock.

The metamorphic rock gets so hot that it melts and becomes magma.

One day, this magma may erupt from a volcano, cool down, and become igneous rock.

volcano erupting

cliffs made of metamorphic rock

Metamorphic rock forms deep inside Earth's crust. Sometimes when the crust moves and cracks, this underground rock gets pushed up onto Earth's surface. Then it may form cliffs or mountains.

Always Changing

The recycling of old rocks to form new rocks is called the rock cycle.

Rocks have been changing from one type to another for billions of years.

In fact, that is what is happening right now—deep beneath your feet!

A small piece of rock might once have been super-hot magma inside Earth. That means it might once have been part of a volcano or been buried deep inside Earth's crust. It might even be so old that a dinosaur once stepped on it!

Deep inside Earth's crust, metamorphic rock melts and becomes **magma**.

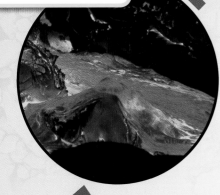

Magma from inside Earth erupts from a volcano as lava.

The lava cools and hardens to form **igneous rock**.

The Rock Cycle

This diagram shows some of the ways in which rocks change to become new rocks.

Igneous rock is broken into tiny pieces by rainwater. The rocky **sediment** is washed into a river and carried to a lake.

Layers of sediment build up in the lake and, over millions of years, form **sedimentary rock**.

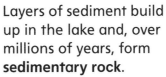

When Earth's crust moves, sedimentary rock is crushed and baked. It changes into **metamorphic rock**.

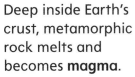

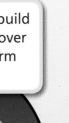

heat   heat

Science Lab

Make a Model of the Rock Cycle

Using modeling clay and some stones, you can make a model showing how rocks are recycled to make new rocks.

You will need:

- Modeling clay
- Stones
- Large piece of cardboard
- Scissors
- Colored and white paper
- Marker

I. Use red clay and stones to make a volcano and lava.

2. Next, use different colored clay to make the three types of rock and some sediment.

igneous rock and sediment

sedimentary rock

metamorphic rock

3. Place your four stages of the rock cycle in a circle on the cardboard.

4. Cut arrows from the colored paper and make labels for your model using the white paper and marker.

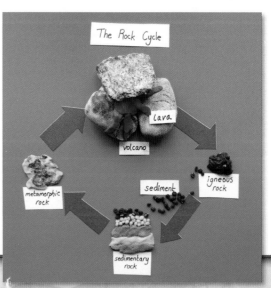

Show your model to your family, friends, or teacher. Explain what is happening in each stage of the rock cycle.

Science Words

igneous (IG-nee-uhss) one of the three main types of rock; granite, gabbro, and basalt are kinds of igneous rock

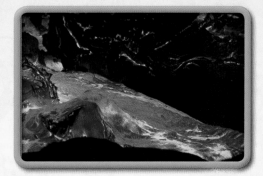

magma (MAG-muh) super-hot liquid rock found deep inside Earth

metamorphic (*met*-uh-MOR-fik) one of the three main types of rock; marble, schist, and quartzite are kinds of metamorphic rock

rock cycle (ROK SYE-kuhl) the process in which one type of rock changes, or is recycled, to become a new type of rock

sediment (SED-uh-muhnt) tiny pieces of rock that have broken away from a larger rock; pebbles and grains of sand are both types of sediment

sedimentary (*sed*-uh-MEN-tuh-ree) one of the three main types of rock; sandstone and conglomerate are kinds of sedimentary rock

Index

Read More

Slade, Suzanne. *The Rock Cycle (Cycles in Nature).* New York: PowerKids Press (2007).

Walker, Sally M. *Rocks (Early Bird Earth Science).* Minneapolis: Lerner (2007).

Zoefeld, Kathleen Weidner. *Rocks and Minerals.* Washington, D.C.: National Geographic (2012).

Learn More Online

To learn more about the rock cycle, visit **www.bearportpublishing.com/Rock-ology**

About the Author

Ellen Lawrence lives in the United Kingdom. Her favorite books to write are those about nature and animals. In fact, the first book Ellen bought for herself, when she was six years old, was the story of a gorilla named Patty Cake that was born in New York's Central Park Zoo.

Answers

Page 11: When lava erupts from a volcano, it cools, hardens, and becomes a mound of igneous rock. The next time the volcano erupts, more lava flows over the mound and turns into rock. Each time the volcano erupts, a new layer of rock is made until the rocky mound becomes a mountain.

Page 15: You can tell that the rock is sedimentary rock because you can see the layers of different sediment that formed the rock.